FOREST BOOKS
CALL YOURSELF ALIVE?

NINA CASSIAN — poet and composer — was born in Galaţi in November 1924. She attended primary school in Braşov and completed her secondary education in Bucharest, where she enrolled as a student of Philology at the University. In 1943 she married Vladimir Colin, a well-known writer of science-fiction and children's tales, but five years later divorced and married Al. J. Ştefănescu, a novelist and short-story writer, who died in 1984. Her first volume of verse, entitled *La Scara 1/1* ('On the Scale 1/1') appeared in 1948 and opened a distinguished career as a writer and translator. In addition to verse, she has composed chamber and symphonic music, and illustrated some of her own books. Her last volume of verse to appear in Romania was *Numărătoarea Inversă* ('Counting Backwards') 1983, and since 1985 she has been living in New York. In 1982 a selection of her poems *Lady of Miracles* was published in California.

ANDREA DELETANT studied languages at Bucharest University. Since coming to England in 1973 she has worked as a freelance lecturer of Romanian. She is co-author of *Romania, A Bibliography* (1985), and has translated several volumes of Romanian verse.

BRENDA WALKER's career has been divided between the arts and education, her university studies being at London and Keele. During the last few years she has devoted herself to poetry in translation and has co-translated with Andrea Deletant a number of Romanian writers.

Nina Cassian

CALL
YOURSELF ALIVE?

the poetry
of
NINA CASSIAN

Translated from the Romanian
by
ANDREA DELETANT
and
BRENDA WALKER

illustrated by
Eugene Mihaescu
and
introduced by
FLEUR ADCOCK

FOREST BOOKS
LONDON ☆ 1988 ☆ BOSTON

PUBLISHED BY FOREST BOOKS
20 Forest View, Chingford, London E4 7AY, U.K.
61 Lincoln Road, Wayland, MA 01788, U.S.A.

First published 1988
Reprinted 1989, 1992, 1994

Typeset in Great Britain by Cover to Cover, Cambridge
Printed in Great Britain by BPCC Wheatons Ltd, Exeter

Translations © Andrea Deletant, Brenda Walker
Illustration & cover design © Eugene Mihaescu

British Library Cataloguing in Publication Data
Cassian, Nina
Call yourself alive?: love poems
of Nina Cassian.
I. Title   II. Deletant, Andrea
III Walker, Brenda
859'.134   PC840.13.A9

ISBN 0–948259–38–8

Library of Congress Catalog Card Number:
87–83570

This translation has been made possible (in part)
through a grant from the Wheatland Foundation.

Contents

AND WHEN SUMMER COMES TO AN END . . .

I LEFT THOSE WALLS . . .

We are indebted to Nina Cassian for her close collaboration and
guidance in these translations. We would also like to thank Fleur
Adcock for the addition of her fine translations of two of the
poems.

Introduction

N INA CASSIAN is a notable phenomenon in Romanian literature: a poet remarkable for the vigour, the sensuality and indeed the savagery of her work, but also an intellectual, a critic, a journalist, and a writer of fiction and of books for children. Side by side with this prolific literary career she has also had a parallel career as a composer, with a sideline in book illustration. But it is as a poet that she is best known, with an established international reputation. She has been publishing poetry for forty years: the earliest poem in this book dates from 1947, the latest from 1987. This selection concentrates on her love poetry, with love being interpreted in its widest sense: not only sexual passion, but love of life, of freedom, and, in the splendidly sensuous final poem, of her own language.

Perhaps the most immediately striking feature of these poems is their startling physicality: Cassian never lets us forget that we have bodies, and that all our living has to be done through them and in them. Mysterious and powerful events happen to people's bodies in her poems. In 'Temptation', which opens this collection, the temptress promises her lover:

> you'll feel your pores opening
> like fish mouths, and you'll actually be able to hear
> your blood surging through all those lanes.

In the tenderly and almost ritualistically erotic 'The First and Last Night of Love' the woman sees 'strange pale herbs dried beneath her hands' where she has touched the man's hair. In 'The Rainmaker' the speaker tells her lover:

> Your arms pour down my body,
> your eyes rinse my throat,
> . . .
> Water-tassels hang from the ends of my fingers.

And in 'Romance' — in which, as so often in Cassian's poems, love has turned to something more like hate — the speaker says:

Forgive me for making you weep,
I should have murdered you,
I should have dragged out your soul
and battered you with it.

There is a good deal of blood in these poems — rather more than is fashionable nowadays, perhaps, but Nina Cassian is not concerned with anything so superficial as fashion.

All the poems I have quoted so far date from the 1960s. In some of her more recent work, Cassian's concern with the physical takes on a new aspect, when she turns to the process of her own ageing. In 'Nude' she writes:

I stroll the beach
with this useless frame
like a piece of scrap . . .

In 'Mud' she sees herself as a crocodile ready to snap, but:

Nothing happens.
I'm just an old woman.

There is despair here, but in a wonderful poem written at about the same time (1983) she has a more positive vision of her ageing self:

In a solar grand old age
cheerful flies pester me
because I smell of honey and sea.

Her awareness of the body's progression through the stages of life also extends backwards, to the years of childhood, in the joyfully celebratory 'Part of a Bird'.

English-speaking readers will find a great deal to enjoy in these translations, but they will partially be deprived of one pleasure: the finely-judged metrical patterns and often rhyming forms of the originals. A great deal of the rhythm and form of Nina Cassian's poetry comes across in Andrea Deletant's and Brenda Walker's sensitive and faithful translations, and the full force of their emotional impact is present, but it is impossible to convey in English the full technical skill of the originals. Cassian has an excellent ear for rhythm — a quality which may possibly be related to her talents as a composer, but has a lot to do with a different expertise in the more subtle and flexible rhythms of spoken language.

The arrangement of the book is thematic rather than chronological, but the dates of the individual poems (bearing in mind that they are only a selection from a lifetime's work) reveal an illuminating pattern: a handful from the 1940s and '50s, a rich gathering from the 1960s, one single example from 1971, and then, after what appears to have been a lull, an abundant harvest from the years since 1980. It is particularly exciting to see so many new poems. They are interspersed throughout the book, but there is also a large cluster of them in the final section, reflecting Nina Cassian's experiences since she left Romania for the United States in 1985. Some express the pain of exile; one or two grieve for the deaths of loved ones:

> The immigration office is not the ideal place
> to keen your dead

some are celebrations of the language she has left behind, as in 'Licentiousness', where she tells of:

> the clitoris in my throat
> vibrating, sensitive, pulsating,
> exploding in the orgasm of Romanian.

But there is also a sense of her looking ahead, tentatively but with a stoical courage, to whatever her new life may bring. At the end of 'The Immigration Department' she writes:

> With the glasses of my loved one
> on my famous nose,
> I'm waiting, waiting,
> for centuries, always waiting
> to be called
> by the clerk.

And in 'Tapestry' we see her stance as that of a figure in a heraldic picture, threatened but still heroic:

> With one foot in the grave
> and the other on the tiger skin
> — that's how I see myself, defeated and triumphant
> in this hunting scene.

It is appropriate that the skin in the image is that of a tiger — an animal which could serve as a symbol for this fierce, lithe, beautifully constructed and uncompromising poetry.

Fleur Adcock

The Literary Career of Nina Cassian:

Publications in Romanian:

POETRY
'Countdown' (1983) — Writers' Union Award)
'Mercy' (1982 — Bucharest Writers' Association Award)
'Lottery Poems' (1971)
'Blood' (1966)
'Dialogue of Wind and Sea' (1958)
'On the Scale 1/1' (1947)

SELECTED POEMS
'Hundred Poems' (1975 — illustrated by the author)
'Show in the Open' (1974)
'Chronophagie' (1970)

FICTION
'Vacation Games' (1984)
'Fictitious Confessions' (1974)

CHILDREN'S BOOKS
'Tigrino and Tigrene' (1964 — Writers' Union Award)
'Fearless Niko' (1952 — State Prize)

Altogether, over 50 books, including 23 volumes of poetry and seven of selected poems, 12 children's books in verse, three volumes of fiction; participation in numerous anthologies; translated into French, German, English, Russian, Italian and Greek; intense journalistic activities included literary, musical and film criticism.

Publications in English:

Blue Apple, translated by Eva Feiler, Cross-Cultural Review Series, Ed. Stanley Barkin (1982)
Lady of Miracles, translated by Laura Schiff, Cloud Marauder Press (Berkeley, 1985)
'Post-Meridian', *The New Yorker* (November 1986)
Four Poems, *The New Yorker* (April 1987)
'Tigrino and Tigrene', a narrative poem for children, *The Lion and the Unicorn*, Brooklyn College (1987)

Translations:

Poems, Paul Celan (1973)
Alle Galgenlieder, Christian Morgenstern (1970)
Poems, Bertolt Brecht (1966)

The Fourth Dimension, Iannis Ritsos (1964)
Trees' Architecture, Iannis Ritsos (1959)
'The Tempest' and 'Hamlet', William Shakespeare

Also translated Moliere, Vladimir Mayakovski, Max Jacob, Guillaume Apollinaire

Grants and Awards

ROMANIA
Writers' Union Awards (1964, 1983)
Writers' Association of Bucharest Award (1982)
State Prize (1952)

UNITED STATES
Participant at the International Writing Program at Iowa
    University (1987)
Fulbright Fellowship (1986)
Yaddo Fellowship (Summer 1986)
Special guest at the 1986 P.E.N. Congress

Readings:

Berkeley, California, with Czeslow Milosz (1986)
New York, P.E.N.-sponsored public discussion with Stanley
    Kunitz (1986)
University of Iowa, Hillel House (1987)
Northern University, Cedar Falls (1987)
New York, Cornelia Street Café (1987)
New York University, two readings (1985–86)

Positions held:

Visiting Professor at New York University (1985–86)

Acknowledgements

La Scara 1/1 (On the Scale 1/1) 1947
Vîrstele Anului (The Years' Ages) 1957
Sarbatorile Ziluice (Daily Festivals) 1961
Să Ne Facem Daruri (Let's Give Gifts to One Another) 1963
Disciplina Harfei (The Discipline of the Lyre) 1965
Sîngele (Blood) 1966
Destinele Paralele (Parallel Destinies) 1967
Ambitus (Ambitus) 1969
Marea Conjugare (The Great Link) 1971
De Indurare (Out of Compassion) 1981
Numarătoărea Inversă (Counting Backwards) 1983

Other poems are from the period 1984–1987, some of which have appeared in poetry journals or newspapers in the U.S.A.

Call Yourself Alive?

Temptation

Call yourself alive? Look, I promise you
that for the first time you'll feel your pores opening
like fish mouths, and you'll actually be able to hear
your blood surging through all those lanes,
and you'll feel light gliding across the cornea
like the train of a dress. For the first time
you'll be aware of gravity
like a thorn in your heel,
and your shoulder blades will ache for want of wings.
Call yourself alive? I promise you
you'll be deafened by dust falling on the furniture,
you'll feel your eyebrows turning to two gashes,
and every memory you have — will begin
at Genesis.

Part of a bird

Even now my breast bone's aching
when I remember how I was running
because the smell of petunias invaded everything.
Ah, God, how warm it was around
my legs, bare, long and free
and evening fell over the sea,
over a crowd, gathered there, and over
the strange deserted pavilion
where we played and I
didn't even think about my ugly head
and other children hadn't noticed it either
because we were all running too fast instead
so the transparent eagle of evening wouldn't get us
and the hum of adults from the street
and the sea, the sea, which threatened (protected)
that final del primo tempo.

It was forever summer, a light summer
a summer of water and sandals, immune
to that alcohol, soon to be called Love,
— and in the deserted pavilion (in vain you'd look for it.
It's either been removed with two fingers
from its ring of earth by War, or by some
useful work, or else forgotten).
We were playing childhood, but, in fact,
I can't remember anyone, I don't think
there was another child apart from me,
because, see, I can only remember
a lonely flight into mystery
staged by the gestures of the sea, I remember
only the happiness, oh God, of leaning
with bare arms and legs on warm stones,
of sloping ground, with grass,
of the innocent air of evening.

4

Flowers smelt dizzily in that place
where, a little above men and women,
who definitely smelt of tobacco,
hot barbecue and beer, I
was running, unaware of my ugly head,
breaking, in fact, the soft head from the flower
and kissing it on the lips
while the sea also smelt more strongly
than now, it was wilder, its seaweed
darker, and cursed the rocks
even more in the way it whipped them.
It wasn't far from home
to that place, I could run there
and back and no one would miss me,
in four steps and eight jumps I was there,
but, first, I stole from fences
feathers of peacocks left between slats,
most beautiful feathers I've not seen since
with the immense blue green eye
and with golden eyelashes so long
that I was holding a whole bird in my hands
not part of one
and I was tearing at feathers
stuck between slats
tearing at something from the mystery
of those fiendish courtyards
and then I was running towards that deserted pavilion
from the edge of the sea
and I was running round it and through it
through derelict rooms
where mad martins battered themselves against walls,
with the ceiling bursting outside and in, as if within me.

I wore a short sleeveless dress
the colour of sand when sun runs out of strength
and in the autumn I should have gone to school,
and the performance of the sea kept breaking my rib cage
to make me more roomy, that's why
my heart was beating and even now the cage in my
                                    chest hurts
at the memory of that beat of the sea
while attempting to enter me
especially at evening when flowers fade

without losing their colour completely,
staying pink with tea, violet with milk,
losing only their stems in the darkness,
floating, beheaded, at a certain height
above the grass which had also vanished.
This is a tremendous memory,
absolutely unforgettable,
the feeling of a light, unchained body,
invulnerable, perfect, my head
just a natural extension of it.
Supervising only its speed and orientation.
Yet I never hurt myself,
I can't remember ever having fallen that summer.
I was light, extremely healthy,
inspired, and if I wasn't flying
it was only because I preferred to run on earth
and not for any other reason.

And after that . . .
What was I saying? Ah, yes, I had long bare legs
and bare slender arms
and in the deserted pavilion there was this strange coolness
as if an invisible sea had breezed through it . . .

And after that . . .
— Where was I? Ah, yes, the flowers full of night . . .
like sacred smoke
and my lonely flight
through gentle and benevolent mysteries . . .

And after that?

The passion

Last night I dreamed of kissing,
fields of ragged carnations
sun stabbing four horizons
with its knives flashing —
from the kisses blood was dripping.

The air, warm as at a stake,
was spreading rusty fluids:
my mouth was full of kisses,
I tried but couldn't escape —
The whole field flickered like a stake.

A forest, its green shield
breathing way off, in the coolness,
ragged carnations at my feet
showed me the distance I must complete
to reach that green shield.

And I stayed in kisses — burning.
clouds chased by cruel sun;
I was never meant to reach them,
those cooling green shields —
I was kissing carnations — burning fields.

Winter event

It was winter in the woods.
Snowdrifts — polar bears —
slumbering in deep lairs.
The forest was raising walls
of black, ferocious branches.

We walked, tired by so many strides
in heavy snow.
A tree, like a giant reindeer
watched us.

Your mouth sealed mine
— and a flame shone beneath my eyelids
as if, with a rustle of fire
a fox had just passed by.

Kisses

Our kisses, hundreds, thousands —
even millions — who knows!
I never counted them:
my fruits, squirrels, carnations,
rivers — my knives!
I could sleep and dream on your mouth,
sing and die there,
again and again;
that mouth — deep harbour
for a night's lodging after a long journey,
reaching it, yet still longing to reach it . . .

They're battles — our kisses —
heavy, slow, hurtful,
where blood, voice and memory all take part.
Oh, how jealous I am of the water you drink
and of words you speak —
of your blue sighs . . .
Jealous of those unjust
partings — of our mouths!

Tiger

You don't have to make that big leap.
Keep on looking at me with those amber eyes.
Wherever I go, what ever I do,
just let those eyes follow me around.
I'll devour them in fistfuls, bite them out of fruit,
see them on every corner of a book,
in the moon, on my left hip,
in the sleep of Saturday's nightmare — ad infinitum.

With so many yellow eyes — I'll have to wear
dark glasses — put my head
under the sea's dark blanket —
but you — no, don't move. Just stare at me,
and keep on staring — with those amber eyes.

God,
How Well I
Remember
the Pain!

The blood

God, how well I remember that pain!
My soul, taken unawares
jerked like a decapitated hen.
Blood spattering everywhere, on the street, the table in
                                        the café,
but mostly over your unconscious hands.
Then, like some prowling monster
my hair dispersed, encircling wine glasses
still as frozen breath,
slashing the air and dancing from side to side,
to fall, executed at your feet.
God, how well I remember — I smiled cruelly,
disfiguring my face to ensure it looked like me,
and then I screamed — just once,
but later, when everyone had left,
lights were out, and they'd wiped
the blood from the tables.

Escape

He locked me in: his love — a prison.
His words and looks — padlocks.
I became blind and mute,
could no longer tell
a curtain from a river;
ashen grass, dead hair invaded me,
dead nails grew on my fingers,
a bluish skin covered my eyes.
I could no longer tell
a bracelet from a muzzle,
a waggon from a cello,
I was speechless — couldn't even answer
the call of the pomegranate seed,
or that kind invitation of frogs in the sunset,
I wasn't even able to say 'hello',
— I lost a lot of friends.

Then suddenly, I noticed
my cheeks had become hollow to the touch,
my hands uneven,
the body was entering its sheath
— and, realising all this, with the speed of disgust
I cut off the dead nails,
excoriated my artificial eyes,
broke the lock
and ran out.
There was no guard.
No one to raise the alarm.
No one called out after me.
No one begged me to return.
Not a soul greeted me.
No one.

Accident

The light collides with the walls, bounces off,
slips into a glass, leaps out choking,
hits my eyeballs with a faint, painful clang,
and then takes a step or two backwards, goes for
your glassy-smooth mouth, and shatters it.
Your mouth is patterned with black veining.
We both have serious injuries.
The light is imitating our blood.

Translated by Fleur Adcock

Of no use

No. You've never needed my gestures
tied up like ribbons round some handle,
or my eyes embroidered on the fixtures,
or my whole playful universe.

You never needed that heavenly bliss
of words — or the absolute yearning
whose pale chisel carved
the stone of moments into the shape of a kiss.

I was no use to you — it was like seasons that pass
in reverse, twos, threes or fours,
like rain trying to fill a glass,
or ruining books when it pours.

A happening

Yesterday I watched an amazing fight
between a woman in love and a man
who wasn't, her hair agitated,
and her mouth interrupted by white teeth.
She talked and talked — he didn't. She talked furiously,
striking expired time with words.
There was no sound of shields.
Time totally disarmed!
She had her arguments, he did not.
He was leaving her for another woman;
He was guilty — so was the other woman,
But the woman who loved was the innocent party.
Her words had a natural nobleness,
The mud of passion left only cast gold.
To avoid her eyes, he looked at his hands —
noticing a certain contrast between them.

It was a ridiculously unfair battle,
the air whistled as if clutching a line
of a thousand arrows never reaching their target.

Everything about them seemed to sink — to decline.

Longing

Oh, my love
heavy anchor
holds me tight:
everything hurts,
mouth — from longing,
eyes — from light.

winds have dropped —
maybe not,
but in the skies
silence reigns,
powerless
heaven sighs.

No more dreams
of steps in snow,
of foxes' traces,
no more flowers —
their hidden souls
sleep in bulbs.

Void. Loneliness . . .
search is pointless —
all that is true
are my doubts:
How real are you?
How real were you?

You distance yourself

You distance yourself swimming with the moon
you distance yourself, sometimes at noon,
and I couldn't care less that your arm
moves heavily under clouds ready for a storm.

And when you rise up on the shore
and like a falling cloak your shoulders lose the sea,
there's no temptation any more —
not one emotion kisses me.

Because you don't love me

I smile, and feel my feeble grin
drip like a blood-streak down my chin
because you don't love me.

I dance, and my heavy hands just trail
like a pair of anchors. I am pale
because you don't love me.

I light a cigarette, and choke
in an Isadora-scarf of smoke
because you don't love me.

Translated by Fleur Adcock

Accident

God protect me from those flashing knives
envy and malice.
Because I wake up bleeding, left huddled on tracks to die,
just as I once found a sheep
far more innocent than I.

Postscript to the end of love

Happy lovers — do exist,
they're always together,
their kiss invigorates, echoes . . .
Listen . . . listen . . .

Immortal couples do exist,
the ones who'll last forever —
their souls, even if parted shaped like
an idea or metaphor.

They'll stay there forever
in that kiss, as if in light thunder.
Listen! Listen! Listen!
Happy lovers — it can happen!

Fairytale

— Why is it that the ugliest of the ugly,
the most hideous of the hideous — wants to be called
                              Prince Charming?
— But, answered the Princess, what befits a disguise?
What if inside that scabby toad there lies bewitched
the wonderful Prince himself?
That's a risk I dare not take.

And the Princess kissed his warts
and took him to bed,
And the scabby toad croaked —
satisfied.

The protector

Again the sea without error
comes forward to meet me
the one who never deceives me
which, with its sweet armour
protects my body
from your ardour.

Like Ana

Once I entered
a house of love with you
and left it fleeing
from misunderstanding,
hating the long street
and starless sky.
Then the first stone fell
on my heart.
Now the building's finished.
No more breathing inside.

Ana was the wife of a master builder in the
Romanian legend Mesterul Manole, in which her sacrifice
was required to ensure the durability of his building.

Capital punishment

I scraped off your smile with nails.
Licked away your eyes. And now
you're nothing but a blank oval, where if I feel like it
I can paint a massacre
or draw a simple flower.
I could even unscrew it — with care —
and leave it lying about close by.

From now on — that's where you start — at the knot in
your tie.

It was a love

If was a love like a chord from Bach,
of such pure gravity . . . Once our movements
had a noble analysed quality
like pieces in a chess game.

Now here you are in total disorder. Alien to laws.
No longer sealing your syllables on my mouth,
or caressing my shoulder. You don't even put your palms
over my forehead flushed with ideas.

I can't lose time like this any longer,
forced to feel pain — ashamed to respond.
I breath deeply: Listen to another chord
that'll take me higher than you — and beyond.

Letters

1.

I'd have written these letters sooner,
but I waited to be free from solitude, I mean
free from that place where trees
stand in prayer
kneeling within themselves,
where rivers flow within themselves,
united in body and soul,
impossible to separate; I've waited
for the spider to leave, the one who
drew himself on my shoulder with a silver pencil.
and now I'm ready — ready to tell you
— I don't love you.

2.

I'm lying on a leaning roof of green tin,
in full sun; I'd slide
if I wasn't riveted by the immense nail of the sun,
and the sky fixes its clouds perpendicularly
to include me in its order; and here I am
an idol of greenish gold, one eye bigger than the other,
and one ear too long — those who sculpted me
were asymmetric — here I am on a sloping roof,
remembering the oblique shadow of your hair,
your entire being, oblique towards the universe and myself,
the angle of your body pointing at some mysterious,
                                        cardinal direction
— and me telling you — I don't love you.

3.

I could have raised a city on your silence.
Nothing moved, I built in a void,
a glittering void, criss-crossed by inspired lightning.
Once I even build a planet
with silk mountains shaped like sleeping birds,
with three cascades into which I threw
seven purple fishes, and I remember
burying an object somewhere in that imagined wall,
an object meant for us — and only for us,
it was the meaning of the planet, its uranium source,
O your silence — but maybe I was deaf,
it could be you were singing, laughing, or howling,
and your silence was just part
of your song, your laughter, your howl.
Perhaps the silence was in fact the planet itself –
                                        overcrowded,
and I wasn't building in a glittering void,
but trying to cover something that already existed
like covering someone who has malaria with a blanket,
just one more blanket, a coat, four pillows,
until he's no longer visible,
— but I don't love you.

4.

I'm writing this fourth letter
in a wooden room, on a wooden table.
Everywhere there's inscriptions in ink,
in indelible pencil or notched with a knife,
names, dates, nightingales, trains,
keys. (You can lock a train
with a key, and you can crush a nightingale
stunned on the track and you can sign your name
and put the date). I'm scared.
Beyond the wooden window frame
the dark sleeve of night's tree pulsates. One night
you waited for me — it was summer —
you'd spread my books on your bed;

and when I entered, I saw myself there,
perhaps it was wrong to replace
the body of paper and wood, with a transient one —
that's how I see it now
when I don't love you.

5.

If you try to hurl
Monday, Tuesday, Wednesday at me —
Monday, Tuesday, Wednesday will rebound
and fall soundlessly back to earth . . .
Thursday, Friday
can't hurt me any more,
nor even leave a trace
like the tiny Japanese umbrella of a vaccination scar.
Thursday and Friday are powerless,
Saturday's powerless as well,
and Sunday — well I no longer know what Sunday means.
— I don't love you!

6.

I look at myself in a mirror.
I can be younger or older,
if I choose I can look like an animal
or a plant or even perhaps
the design plans of some flying machine.
Once you flowed like volcanic lava
over all my forms — no, I wasn't petrified,
the proof is in the mirror,
the merging seasons,
mutations, and this hand of mine
which once propped up your eyes
to prevent them falling from their sockets
like two enormous tears,
this hand of mine which now writes:
Look — I don't love you.

7.

I'm writing my seventh letter leaning on a grey wall.
I remember your oblique mouth,
the embrace you used to strangle me,
the splendour of the ballroom
where our mistakes fell in love
with each other at first sight,
the way you let the hour-glass break
allowing time to abandon me suddenly,
and I remember your movements
that sentenced me to death;
so I lean on the grey wall of a courtroom;
but I have nothing to say except — I don't love you.
And I'll say it again and again — I don't love you.
That's all. I don't love you.
I don't love you.

Donna miraculata

Since you left me I seem more beautiful
Like a corpse lighting up the darkness.
My eye, now more fixed and spherical,
Can no longer be seen — or my carcass.

Or the rags of my hands upon objects,
Or my useless walking disfigured by longing,
— Just your cruelty on my perfect temples,
Like a halo of decay that's shining.

Morning exercises

I wake up and say: I'm through.
It's my first thought at dawn.
What a nice way to start the day
with such a murderous thought.

God, take pity on me
— is the second thought, and then
I get out of bed
and live as if
nothing had been said.

Lemur I

I kissed the blood on those soles of yours,
those stick-like arms of yours,
while your death-grin
bit into my heart.

Now, for no apparent reason, you're far off and in harmony
with the might of the beyond.
It's a pose you take
to add to my humiliation.

You'd do better if you helped me fight night
and then leave me to howl
that low-pitched, high-pitched fright
of a terrified animal.

Lemur II

It stirs all round me —
Lemur,
the soul of the dead.
It airs my skin
still damp from the spit of the sea.
It cools my blood.
Cures me of all five senses.

All I ever do is love you, yearn for you.
The Sagittarius has vanished.
Thinner, sharper,
only the platinum tip of his arrow
points towards your abstraction.

Consolation

No one holds me tight anymore
to enfold me back into his rib.
There's no one to wipe the rust from my wrists
left by handcuffs.
Kisses are abolished
by order from above.

At my feet — consolation,
— a bitch
with an Assyrian profile.

Daily execution

I feel you under my tongue
like some homoeopathic pill
melting in saliva,
my most intimate fluids
my plasma,
and my ectoplasm.

My love — so unheard of —
for so long never again heard of . . .

— (these are my last thoughts,
when a thousand volts of longing
shake my being
— electric chair.)

Stained-glass window

I came here to be with you in winter's crystal —
as in a stained-glass window,
ancient couples of kings and queens.
I counted the even trees on the way to your home.
The snow was sumptuous, magic, like in a ballad.

I knocked at the gate. Its wood was cold.
Everywhere absence — like a new
and total winter. The sweet prince
— nowhere . . . with both hands
I took snow and drank
that white place you'd never crossed.

Flowers of death

Lilies, flowers of death
breathe in my hair, my eyelids,
filling me with their aroma —
homogenous — terrestrial,
bringing me closer, closer
to you my rigid, rock-like dead,
tearing, separating me from my cells
and from everything that moves.

Us two

My God, what a dream I had:
the two of us, more passionate than ever,
making love like the first couple on earth . . .
— and we were so beautiful, naked and wild,
and both dead.

A dream of drought

Water's getting dearer.
I'd better learn
To swim in dust
And drink mud.

Birds leave in the autumn
And don't return in the spring.

Blue cloth's getting dearer.
I'd better get used
To wearing black.

Even fish scales of any size
Have registered a rise!

A very simple poem

Over the sands a wave of craving.
Traces of the sea are drying on my face.

A last sheep tugs inanely at the last grass,
Summer's wine and blood no longer boil.

Yesterday's wound which seemed so deep
Has closed overnight. — My flesh is still young!
But I don't heal from the century's wound, the wound of
                                      the world,
Those fragile verses,
Antimus?
Posthumus?

Haunting

A mat of dead butterflies at my feet,
dead and soft.
(For them rigor mortis doesn't exist)
I'm very healthy,
I've taken my liver out,
removed my lungs,
I've even taken away my heart
so there's no more pain.

Being a ghost
is a solution
I coldly recommend.

And When
Summer Comes
to an End . .

And when summer comes to an end . . .

And when summer comes to an end
it's like the world coming to an end.
Wilderness and terror — everywhere!

Days shrink
till all dignity's gone.
Wet slabs of cloth
drape our bodies:
dejected coats.
And then we shiver, stumbling
into the holes of Winter Street
on the corner of Decline . . .

What's the good of living
with the idea of Spring
— dangerous as any Utopia?

The first and last night of love

1.

Wolves, snow, and the amazement of being together
made them very silent. Among the trees
their old bodies lay in wait — old eyes
with old glances, refusing to believe they'd ever been
forgotten — were they — forgotten?
Weren't they merely a succession,
wearing numerous heads,
always agreeing and nodding in unison,
weren't their arms more infinite,
and far more significant than those of
familiar and frightening oriental statues.
In the silence one could hear their soft murmuring,
a dispute in the intimacy of cells,
while the night strangled pursuers
with her firm grip.

2.

They were aware of one thing only: the start
of their first night of love. They'd entered
a set specially designed, a room
where sinister paintings had been removed,
a cat with a mouse in her womb, a still-life
with sliced fowl — silvery stripes on the walls
marked a distinguished yet obvious absence —
and there were a few pieces of furniture, plus the
                                        nuptial bed
with its immense cover the colour of water.
They were together — could touch each other, mix
hair in the same glass, skin in the same scent.
They could chase flames on the curve of their hips,
thrusting kisses where bones met.
But first they should have got rid of the bundles of
death we all carry
placing them carefully on the green tiles of the hearth.

3.

Deeply moved he lay at her feet —
in silence. She was watching his hair where
strange pale herbs dried beneath her hands.
She also touched his heart, and was startled
by the urgent rhythms — as if syllables
ran outside the words, and the touch
of his coat still felt strange to her
and beneath it, the shape of his shoulders and chest.
This time no-one had followed them —
except themselves — abandoned and annexed to themselves
and so, numerous in body and soul, they rested
in a motionless dance.

4.

Time and time again she emerged from herself,
until perhaps nakedness,
helped him find his way to her
through the crowd.
He came slowly, undulating, unknown, always nearer,
always meeting, and it seemed that he always
made this journey towards her, through her, to her —
so climbing towards him, she passed on through to find
                                                    herself
somewhere beyond them both, yet still meeting him
coming towards her, approaching her, always coming,
                                        always meeting,
— and a great continuity kept them together
till the cry.

5.

Late, after midnight, she fell asleep — he didn't.
In her sleep, she heard him breathing a long way off,
like a river at the end of an immense and indifferent
plain. So as not to disturb her, he didn't move, but she,
in moving, touched

his shoulder, familiar now, but cold with night
and from time to time, as he looked at her, she foresaw
the cold night of his gaze.
Bodies returning to bodies, much too young
to become memories, much too old
to misunderstand such beauty.
It was a strong night, a symbol
inhaled very slowly.
The dead held their breath.

6.

Then they'd packed everything and fled,
deserting night, and the set in which
the paintings had slowly reappeared; first
the phosphorescent contour of the cat,
then the contour of the mouse within her, then blood
the screaming blood of birds, the knives glistened.
They ran, ran, but this time
followers could not be stopped. The dead
once awake, surrounded them
at first invisible but then she was suddenly aware
of a black thread wound
like a thin scar round her left hand, and he
felt his lips mysteriously covered in blood.
They spoke words of love, out loud — but neither heard.
They could no longer hear their own voices, but saw
word shapes freezing in the air.
Then they shouted with eyes — brows —
but neither heard. Their bodies
began to circle slowly, moving away.
The dead became visible, they stumbled into them,
and when lost amongst them, lost themselves —
never to find each other ever again.

7.

And the wolves died,
and the snows melted.
Everything had happened so fast
you'd never have guessed
what had gone on there with heads — with limbs. Even
if you'd asked, they couldn't have told you
where or how those strange nocturnal face stains had
                                        appeared.
In fact how could they know, since by day their faces
were clean and pale, they'd wonder, they'd glance
                                        fleetingly
in the mirror, but too fast to notice
night's greedy eye in the far upper corner, they'd wonder —
then refuse to be questioned any more.

Bread and wine

We said there'd be a celebration . . .
There wasn't.
And so I dressed for no apparent
reason in the height of fashion.

I waited for you till dawn.
All night I waited.
In the carafe — stagnant wine,
on the tables — stale bread.

And when day came upon the land
— and I knew it would remain there —
I took the flowers from my hair
with a withered hand.

I wanted to stay in September

I wanted to stay in September
on that pale deserted beach.
I wanted to cram myself
with ashes from my unfaithful cranes
and let the slow, heavy wind
fall asleep in my long hair
like water in the trawl:
One night, I wanted to light
a cigarette, whiter than the moon,
with no one around — just the sea
with its solemn, hidden force;
I wanted to stay in September,
witnessing the passage of time,
with one hand in the trees — the other
in the greying sand, to slip
along with summer into autumn

But it seems my fate's cast
for more dramatic exits,
fated to be uprooted from landscapes
with an unprepared soul,
as I'm fated to quit loving
while still hired to love.

The rainmaker

You're him — the rainmaker.
Your arms pour down my body,
your eyes rinse my throat,
your mouth blossoms on my hip
like a moist blue flower.
You tore off the golden ring
that wedded me to drought,
that ring of arid gold
engraved with ashen thorns.
The restlessness of harvest swells my breasts.
Water-tassels hang from the ends of my fingers.
Faint thunder travels in and through us.

Vacation

The sea abandoned two blue bodies on the shore.
They could have generated many stars.
They were — they told us — our bodies,
and good folk tried to lay us out.

The blue colour wasn't easy to remove.
The night came — colour killer —
The moon hurried, like that old new moon,
to pour liquor quickly before thirsty dawn took her.

Finally, discoloured, we woke — and loved.
An orange monocle rose from the sea's waistcoat.
High time to look like all the others.
We boiled in oil the last aristocratic fishes.

And in the town of rare trees and light bulbs
dressed alike and put on spectacles.

Romance

Forgive me for making you weep,
I should have murdered you,
I should have dragged out your soul
and battered you with it.

I should have watched your blood
flow, surge after surge,
and left your puny, pock-marked self alone,
not caressed your eyes, nostrils and mouth.

Forgive me for making you suffer,
I should have terrified you,
But I'm not God — the avenger
— only his creation of dust.

Nude

Hips, belly, boobs
— for what?
I stroll the beach
with this useless frame
like a piece of scrap — the last on earth,
me and some sad-looking sheep.
(Once we grazed together
the golden parsley of the stars.)
The sky's empty
Tomorrow's night.

How did I come to lose the moon . . . ?

How did I come to lose the moon
where I bathed every year
to regain my youth?
It was lost like precious oil;
trickling through finger tips,
seeping into sand.

And look, the great shadow crosses
my wrinkled skin,
the great shadow crosses,
circles under my eyes
gather out of nowhere,
and yet another circle
like a black moon
comes beneath my saddened breast.

Perpetual rhythm

The woodcutter
asks the time, talks about the weather.

Asks how long he's got
so he can tell
how long I've got.
I reply — it's early
I don't know when my time'll be up.

The woodman knows.
He's seen it all before
while knocking up a coffin.
— Who for?

My crimes

A stifled sun . . .
forgive me, forgive me . . .
Where I've sown
bitter herbs have grown.
Whatever I've sewn
is now frayed and torn,
and where I've poured clear wine
innocent glasses
have cracked and crumbled.
Forgive me, forgive me.

* * *

In a solar grand old age
cheerful flies pester me
because I smell of honey and sea.
I bury myself gradually and greedily.
My sumptuous greenish hair
protects me from the looks
of the few aggressors
coming from the sea
on long ships lacquered with blood.

In the shelter of my age
I hear my nails growing.

That's about it

More and more often,
more and more painfully,
I remember something else:
how a child once pulled faces at me,
how all the addresses where I lived
had names of plants,
the smell of my drawing book
and, after that,
the atmosphere of a kiss which embraced me,
I walked and breathed kisses to suffocation,
and, after that, sacks with the dead
which I carried on my back
and still carry
— well, yes that's it,
that's about it,
that's what you'd call my life,
the one in the skin of the sea,
in the garment of the grass,
in the curse of not speaking,
in the labour of not creating.

I
Left Those
Walls

I left those walls

I've left those walls
covered in my blood
(it was a terrible massacre).
Now I fly over the town
not like a bride
near her bridegroom violinist,
but like a winged nightmare
with a complete biography of dirty feathers.

I should have left earlier,
before being exterminated
by loneliness
and the chaotic axes
of those choppers of people,
of head hunters.
I should have —
But who knows
how much one can endure?
I was waiting cautiously, and still waiting
the day passes, life passes,
and in our bones,
black worms burrow canals
in our eyes,
the milk of light goes sour,
and our tongues swell
like mumbling mushrooms.
But I've left those walls
and that house of massacres.
Now I fly,
a nightmare bird
who all can hear whirring
yet no-one believes
is really me.

The cold

Cold. Necessary cold
raising the first protruberances; the mountains,
sons and daughters of cold,
tamed then to the first vegetal feeling,
to the first call of an eye,
to the first unbalanced ape
— to humanity.

When the snake's tongue parts
— it's getting cold.
Cold is the result of divergence.
I stretch my hand — and something withdraws
or, if I still touch it
contracts itself abruptly
becoming dark and crouched.
Something moves away leaving a trace of cold,
something always abandons its place
leaving behind a cold space,
something separates from something
in the great analytical moment.

Cold has no shadow
His contour doesn't allow him this evasion.
Shadow is form's feeling.
Cold has no feeling.
Cold has no feelings.
He's immutable, self-centred, he doesn't communicate.

On the table — two glasses
and two parallel spoons.
At the table, two parallel people
watching the street.
A man and a woman
or a woman and a man
— you can't tell
because they don't attract one other.
I dilate myself — to fill up the conventional space
                                    between people.
To take revenge, they try to crush me, anyway,
they have to touch me and, if I step away
they collide with each other, touch each other,

having no choice, they yell at one another,
and so end up addressing each other,
willy-nilly they notice themselves and their similarities,
and that happens at the surface of the massacre, in the open,
or higher still at the level of conscience
— who could name the place where something begins to
                                        change?

Cold's lifestyle produces a strange impression of order.
In fact, under conventional lines,
I suspect a wild movement,
everyone has teeth clenched into another's carotid,
nails thrust into another's flesh;
under the plate of cold
a daily massacre takes place,
a hunger which has lost its meaning,
a competition which has lost all sense,
and the more the turmoil turns vicious,
the more distinguished conventional lines appear,
like a draught traced with chalk on a blackboard
which looks so much like a ghost.

Cold between stars, people,
cold bisecting couples with lines
— and in between, an infinite net of conventions
(reminders of ideas and sentiments
or projections of ideas and sentiments
— things are mixed up), as for the laws,
the laws flow in an invisible, implacable way, beyond
                                cold and warmth,
so that this small, circumstantial law — the convention —
seems suddenly friendly and sailing — after all
she is the one who asks for our handshake,
for uttering 'good day' and 'good night',
she, the convention, the pale, sweet sister of the law,
making it easier for us, if not to live,
at least, to survive.

Face to face

I waited for this moment when, face to face
we are travelling toward a destination which separates us,
face to face, with our features, violently reciprocated,
with our hands exhausted by blood,
not daring to kiss, with our clothes not daring to turn red,
with our mouths deserted by that word
that brings day and night into the world.
So, here we are, face to face, becoming more and more
                                        estranged,
alienating ourselves with our whole capacity of
                                    misunderstanding,
in a true species — adversity — so that,
when the train jerks us into each other's arms
we have the revelation of death
as, probably the mammoths had
when they leapt into the next era.

Mud

The scales which cover me
are the colour of earth
like a crocodile
adapted to the surrounding mud,
motionless — eyes appearing asleep,
inside — ferocious.

The insignificant animal ought to beware of me.
Look at it hopping around,
its hairy muzzle touching my back.
I feel my jaws clenching
ready to open
into that great murderous yawn.

Nothing happens.
I'm just an old woman.

Triumphant being

In the light of pine trees,
in the smell of the sun
and made rhythmical
by dripping from the eaves,
— at first sight, I'm
a triumphant being,
at second,
a piece of sad flesh — *hélas!* —
left over on the acrid plate of the world
when the great feast has past
and the great devourers
consume other game.

Vowel

A clean vowel
is my morning,
Latin pronounciation
in the murmur of confused time.
With rational syllables
I'm trying to clear the occult mind
and promiscuous violence.
My linguistic protest
has no power.
The enemy is illiterate.

Ceremony

My poems boil
in cauldrons, in pots, in perculators.
The whole house smells of poetry
just like autumn,
as if my soul
were jam,
sticky, shiney, slimey,
— a muddy memory of a plum.

Tapestry

With one foot in the grave
and the other on the tiger skin
— that's how I see myself, defeated and triumphant
in this hunting scene.

Winter festivals

Hanging from the ceiling
by a silver thread —
four sheep
and six small ships.
At the slightest breath
sheep, ships,
turn in the air
with a delicate tinkling
and it could be Christmas
(and indeed it is Christmas)
in mid-America
where my weak being
rotates without air,
without delicate tinkling,
hung from the ceiling . . .

Anniversary

The date of your death draws near.
I stand bare-breasted in the light,
I can see my womb pulsating,
my womb where your seeds never germinated,
my thighs which so many times gripped
the branch of your body . . .
It's a continuous unreality
which shoves me through the world
and which this time
is called Kismet.
Kismet?
A Turkish resonance in the south of New York state?
. . . But, since Kismet means destiny,
everything is explained.

Fog

Fog obliterating colours,
greying characters;
If I dig the fog with my hands
I'll come across other hands digging towards me.
My ghost would bump into another ghost
and make love
like the invisible man with his invisible wife.
The beach has retreated into non-existence.
Only the huge wave of the shore
thunders in a foreign language
or maybe returns the syllables of Demosthenes
(but sharper, more imperiously).
When the fog falls
I could be anywhere on earth or in heaven.
I feel in the censorship of an eternal verse.

The immigration department

Me with my pen
hoping the ink won't run out
before I register a new defeat.
Look I'm waiting — as I've waited year after year —
for them to deny me
the right to poetry, to an orange,
perhaps even the status to be human.
My identity — more and more uncertain.
In vain I keep writing my name on books,
on scores, in the right-hand corner of an idea,
my name — a convention;
my being — an abstraction;
distinguishing marks — none.
(Oh yes: a rash of pride on my left cheek . . .)
in the end
the denials which besiege me
define my very being
just like the knife thrower
who gets his victim's perfect outline
from the knives he throws at the board.

So
I've no chance
although I'm wearing
the protective glasses of my loved one
(things have outlived him:
his purple jacket brilliantly patterned,
the absurd hat bought on Barbe's Boulevard,
the gloves lost then found,
and of course the photographs,
three of them carried on me always:
the one where he strangles me, smiling,
and me with a happy smile
letting myself be strangled.
The one in which he wears the glasses I'm wearing now
looking at me with slight admonishment
sometimes with benevolent irony.

Finally the one where he only looks
at something that looks at him
inviting him politely to leave the world . . .)

The immigration office is not the ideal place
to keen your dead,
but I can't control it
and the public eye me
as they would a miserable creature . . .
which in fact I am
if you take into account my loss
of parents, of pair, of pastures,
of shared pillow, of shared passion . . .

The clerk won't be convinced
of my metaphors;
I almost long to be refused
my respectful application to poetry
to conform with my destiny
familiarized with its commandment
(hope unbalances me).
With the glasses of my loved one
on my famous nose,
I'm waiting, waiting,
for centuries, always waiting
to be called
by the clerk.

Prayer

If you really exist — show up
as a bear, a goat, a pilot,
come with eyes, mouth, voice,
— demand something from me,
force me to sacrifice myself,
take me in your arms, protect me from above,
feed me with the seventh part of one fish,
hiss at me, reanimate my fingers,
refill me with aromas, with astonishment
— resurrect me.

Licentiousness

Letters fall from my words
like teeth might fall from my mouth.
Lisping? Stammering? Mumbling?
Or the last silence?
Please God take pity
on the roof of my mouth,
on my tongue,
on my glotis,
on the clitoris in my throat
vibrating, sensitive, pulsating,
exploding in the orgasm of Romanian.

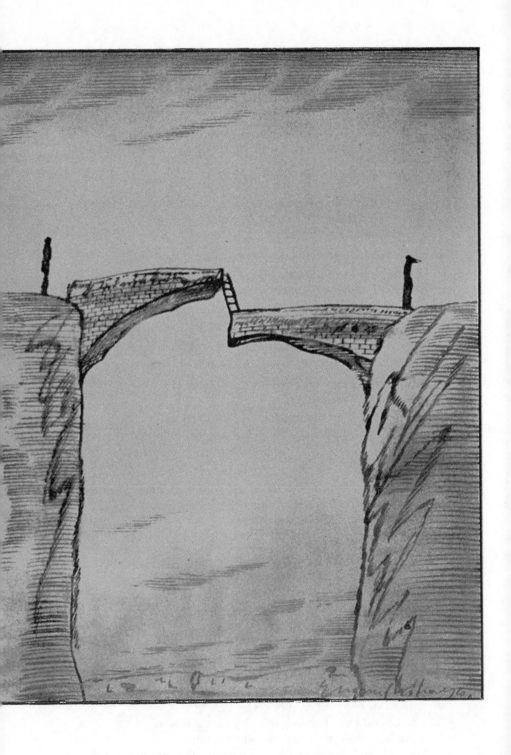

FOREST BOOKS

Special Collection

THE NAKED MACHINE Selected poems of Matthías Johannessen. Translated from the *Icelandic* by Marshall Brement. (Forest/ Almenna Bokáfélagid)
0 948259 44 2 cloth £7.95   0 948259 43 4 paper £5.95   96 pages

ON THE CUTTING EDGE Selected poems of Justo Jorge Padrón. Translated from the *Spanish* by Louis Bourne.
0 948259 42 6 paper £7.95   176 pages

ROOM WITHOUT WALLS Selected poems of Bo Carpelan. Translated from the *Swedish* by Ann Borne.
0 948259 08 6 paper £6.95   144 pages. Illustrated

CALL YOURSELF ALIVE? The love poems of Nina Cassian. Translated from the *Romanian* by Andrea Deletant and Brenda Walker. Introduction by Fleur Adcock.
0 948259 38 8 paper £5.95   96 pages. Illustrated

RUNNING TO THE SHROUDS Six sea stories of Konstantin Stanyukovich.
Translated from the *Russian* by Neil Parsons.
0 948259 04 3 paper £5.95   112 pages. Illustrated.

East European Series

FOOTPRINTS OF THE WIND Selected poems of Mateya Matevski. Translated from the *Macedonian* by Ewald Osers. Introduction by Robin Skelton.
0 948259 41 8 paper £6.95   96 pages. Illustrated

ARIADNE'S THREAD An anthology of contemporary Polish Women poets. Translated from the *Polish* by Susan Bassnett and Piotr Kuhiwczak.
0 948259 45 0 paper £6.95   96 pages.

POETS OF BULGARIA An anthology of contemporary Bulgarian poets.
Edited by William Meredith. Introduction by Alan Brownjohn.
0 948259 39 6 paper £6.95   112 pages.

THE ROAD TO FREEDOM Poems by Geo Milev. Translated from the *Bulgarian* by Ewald Osers.
UNESCO collection of representative works.
0 948259 40 X paper £6.95   96 pages. Illustrated.

STOLEN FIRE Selected poems by Lyubomir Levchev.
Translated from the *Bulgarian* by Ewald Osers.
Introduction by John Balaban.
UNESCO collection of representative works.
0 948259 04 3 paper £5.95   112 pages. Illustrated.

AN ANTHOLOGY OF CONTEMPORARY ROMANIAN POETRY
Translated by Andrea Deletant and Brenda Walker.
0 9509487 4 8 paper £5.00   112 pages.

GATES OF THE MOMENT Selected poems of Ion Stoica.
Translated from the *Romanian* by Brenda Walker and
Andrea Deletant. Dual text with cassette.
0 9509487 0 5 paper £5.00   126 pages   Cassette £3.50 plus VAT

SILENT VOICES An anthology of contemporary Romanian women
poets. Translated by Andrea Deletant and Brenda Walker.
0 948259 03 5 paper £6.95   172 pages.

EXILE ON A PEPPERCORN Selected poems of Mircea Dinescu.
Translated from the *Romanian* by Andrea Deletant and
Brenda Walker.
0 948259 00 0 paper £5.95.   96 pages. Illustrated.

LET'S TALK ABOUT THE WEATHER Selected poems of Marin Sorescu.
Translated from the *Romanian* by Andrea Deletant and
Brenda Walker.
0 9509487 8 0 paper £5.95   96 pages.

THE THIRST OF THE SALT MOUNTAIN Three plays by Marin Sorescu
(Jonah, The Verger, and the Matrix).
Translated from the *Romanian* by Andrea Deletant and
Brenda Walker.
0 9509487 5 6 paper £6.95   124 pages. Illustrated

VLAD DRACULA THE IMPALER A play by Marin Sorescu.
Translated from the *Romanian* by Dennis Deletant.
0 948259 07 8 paper £6.95   112 pages. Illustrated.

Fun Series

JOUSTS OF APHRODITE Erotic poems collected from the Greek
Anthology Book V.
Translated from the *Greek* into modern English by Michael Kelly.
0 948259 05 1 cloth £6.95   0 948259 34 5 paper £4.95   96 pages.